Diversity

by Jennifer Earnshaw

PEARSON

Glenview, Illinois
Boston, Massachusetts
Chandler, Arizona
New York, New York

Illustrations
2 Adam Benton; 7, FP2, FP5 Precision Graphics; 15 Peter Bollinger

Photographs
Every effort has been made to secure permission and provide appropriate credit for photographic material. The publisher deeply regrets any omission and pledges to correct errors called to its attention in subsequent editions.

Photo locators denoted as follows: Top (T), Center (C), Bottom (B), Left (L), Right (R), Background (Bkgd)

CVR: Audrey Snider-Bell/Shutterstock; FP2TL: Prudkov/Fotolia; FP2BL: Jon E Oringer/Shutterstock; FP2BR: Photos.com/Getty Images; 1: Joze Maucec/Shutterstock; 3: Jupiterimages/Photos.com/Getty Images; 4: Pablo Hidalgo/Shutterstock; 5: Kirill Ilchenko/Shutterstock; 6: Corbis; 8: Markus Bormann/Fotolia; 9L: Kaschibo/Shutterstock; 9R: Nichkann/Fotolia; 10TR: Joze Maucec/Shutterstock; 10BR: Audrey Snider-Bell/Shutterstock; 10L: Zachary Bowden/Alamy; 11: Photos.com/Getty Images; 12: Maggymeyer/Fotolia; 13: Jon E Oringer/Shutterstock; 14: Getty Images; FP3T: Pablo Hidalgo/Shutterstock; FP3B: Raymond Kasprzak/Shutterstock; FP4T: Ethan Daniels/Shutterstock; FP4C: Dorling Kindersley Ltd.; FP4B: Joze Maucec/Shutterstock.

ISBN-13: 978-0-328-61749-4
ISBN-10: 0-328-61749-0

10 18

Environmental Changes

All living things live in an environment where their needs are met. An **environment** is all of the conditions surrounding a living thing.

Environments change as the food supply and other things change. For example, a population of millipedes lives in an environment with dead plants. As the number of millipedes rises, each millipede will have less food, water, and space.

Some millipedes will die. Others will move away. Then the remaining millipedes will again have enough resources. When the population grows large enough, the cycle will start over. Living things must change the way they live to survive in a changing environment.

A population of ants lives in this tree. As the number of ants gets larger, there may not be enough space or food for them.

Slow Changes

Sometimes environments change very slowly. For example, the climate in an area may change over thousands of years. This happened in the Sahara in Africa. It has been wet and dry there in the past.

Seasons change slowly every year. This gives some animals enough time to grow winter fur. Plants have time to grow new leaves for the summer.

The continents have moved over millions of years. For example, Antarctica used to be much closer to the equator. It had a much warmer climate before it moved.

Rocks are slowly broken down by the weather. Plants and animals break down rocks too. The rocks become part of the soil.

Lichens are living things. Orange lichens on this rock are slowly breaking it down. Over time, the rock will become soil.

Fast Changes

Natural events can also change an environment quickly. Hurricanes, floods, fires, volcanic eruptions, and earthquakes are natural events that cause fast changes. A hurricane's strong winds can rip up trees and flatten plants. Heavy rains and big waves can flood a coast. When lightning strikes a tree, it can start a forest fire. The fire may burn much of what is in its path.

When one of these natural events happens, it affects plants and animals. Fast changes may force a species, or a kind of living thing, to leave an area. Resources like food and shelter may no longer be there.

The eruption of a volcano can quickly kill living things. But it can also add nutrients to the soil that other living things can use.

Changes Caused by Organisms

Organisms may change their own environment as they feed, grow, and build their homes. For example, locusts are insects that travel in large groups called swarms. A swarm of locusts can eat all the plants in large fields and destroy crops. After locusts pass through, the area is changed. An area that was once full of plants will be empty.

Plants also cause changes. They affect the quality of the air. They take in carbon dioxide and give off oxygen into the air. Most living things need oxygen to live.

A swarm of locusts can be many kilometers long. Locusts can eat thousands of pounds of plants.

Human Activities

Humans are one of the main causes of changes in the environment. People build dams to get energy. They clear forests to get wood and to plant crops. People change the environment when they build buildings and roads. They change the environment when they burn fuel.

There are many ways people can limit the changes they make to the environment. For example, they can build tunnels under roads where there is heavy traffic. The tunnels let animals cross the roads safely.

Farmers change the land to plant crops.
They may clear trees and take away rocks.

Birds and other fast animals can escape a fire.

Some plants store food in tuber roots. They use the food to grow again after a fire.

Slower animals may survive a fire if they live underground.

A forest fire can both harm and help an environment.

Adapting to Change

Changes that hurt some living things may help others. A forest fire destroys trees and bushes. The bushes and trees help protect the soil from being washed away by rainwater. The fire adds smoke and carbon dioxide to the air. It destroys the habitats of many animals.

A forest fire may also help living things in a forest. It clears away dead and dying plants. This makes room for new plants to grow. The ashes left over from the fire put nutrients back into the soil.

In any environment, resources are limited. The struggle of living things for the same resources is called **competition.**

Survival

For any kind of living thing, there are differences between individuals. One plant may have deeper roots than other plants. This plant will be able to reach deeper into the soil to get water. One animal may run a little faster than others of its kind. This animal has a better chance of surviving an attack by another animal.

Only those living things that survive will reproduce. They will pass along to their offspring the traits that helped them to survive. For example, a resurrection plant can survive very dry seasons. It is able to dry up without dying. Look at the two pictures of the resurrection plant. The dried-up, brown plant was given water. A day later it became green.

These pictures show the same resurrection plant before and after getting water.

Animal Adaptations

Animals have adaptations for survival. The adaptations help them react to sudden threats. An **adaptation** is a change that allows a living thing to survive better in its environment. The blue-ringed octopus is usually pale. When a predator comes too close, it turns bright yellow with blue rings. Other animals might react to danger by running, flying, or using poison.

Some changes happen too slowly to affect animals. For example, the amount of salt in the oceans changes very slowly over time. Different species of animals in the ocean change over time to adapt to this slow change.

blue-ringed octopus before and after color changes

Life-Cycle Differences

Different animals have different life cycles. These life cycles help animals survive in their environments. For example, many birds lay their eggs in the spring. The young birds then have many months of good weather. Food is easy to find. These things help them grow into adults.

Physical Traits

Useful changes in the body of an animal are called structural adaptations. For example, animals that hunt may have eyes on the front of the head. This helps them know how far away their prey is. Animals that are hunted may have eyes on the sides of the head. This helps them see where a predator might be coming from.

The okapi's long tongue helps it reach leaves.

A sea urchin's spines protect it.

The gecko's foot helps it climb.

Each animal has structural adaptations that help it survive in its environment.

Genes are like instructions for how an animal grows. Genes of a bear may give the bear thicker fur. The thicker fur may help the bear to survive a cold winter. The offspring of the bear will likely inherit this useful structural adaptation.

Extinction

A species cannot survive if it does not adapt to changes or move to a new environment. Some species cannot move to a new environment. For example, plants cannot pull themselves up by the roots and walk to another place. If a species does not adapt or move away, its population will get smaller. When a species has no members left that are alive, it becomes an **extinct species.**

This is a dodo bird. It lived on an island until other animals were brought there. The dodo bird could not defend itself and became extinct.

Behavioral Adaptations

Atlantic ghost crabs are born knowing how to dig deep holes in the beaches where they live. This behavior is in the genes they inherit from their parents. It is a behavioral adaptation passed from parent to offspring.

Behavioral adaptations help animals survive. Such adaptations are sometimes called instincts. They affect what an animal does around other animals. Some animals, like the ghost crab, have an instinct to dig into the ground to hide from predators.

Not all behaviors are instincts. Some behaviors are learned. For example, lion cubs learn to hunt by watching their parents.

The lion cubs practice hunting while playing with one another.

Plant Adaptations

Plants compete to use the same resources. When an environment changes, these resources may become limited. Plants with the best adaptations are more likely to survive. Adaptations develop over many generations.

Plants receive genes from their parents. Genes are like instructions for how the plant grows. Most plants are very similar to their parents. A plant will have the same type of flowers and leaves as its parents.

A plant may be a bit different from its parents. Some plants may be a little taller than their parents. Some may have different-colored flowers. Plants may also have a mutation. This is a random change in a gene.

A mangrove tree can take in air through roots above the water. This adaptation helps the plant survive.

Natural Selection

If a mutation is helpful, the plant will survive in its environment. The plant will have a better chance to have offspring. It will pass on its genes to its offspring. If a mutation is harmful, the plant will be less likely to survive. It will also be less likely to have offspring. Over time, small mutations can add up to a big change. This process is called natural selection. Natural selection helps all living things adapt to survive.

Life-Cycle Differences

The life cycles of plants are adapted to their environments. For example, morning glory vines grow very fast in warm weather. They produce flowers and seeds and then die before the cold arrives again. Other plants live through the winter. They do not produce flowers or seeds until spring.

Cherry trees grow where the winter is cold. They produce flowers in spring and cherries in summer.

Physical Characteristics

Changes in plant parts can help a plant survive. For example, coconuts are large seeds. Some coconuts float better than others. A coconut seed that floats well may go farther than other seeds and have less competition for resources. The seed may survive and grow into a palm tree.

Succession

When an environment changes, living things also change. Succession is the predictable order of changes in communities after there is an environmental change. New conditions allow new communities to move into the environment. Bare land might become grassland. Grassland will become shrubs. Shrub land will become a forest. Communities grow and replace one another until there is a stable community.

The pictures show the same place at different times. Over time, a lake area can become a forest.

Glossary

adaptation   a change that allows a living thing to survive better in its environment

competition   the struggle of living things for the same limited resources

environment   all of the conditions surrounding a living thing

extinct species   a species that has no members left that are alive